# Music and
# Singing

# Ready, Steady, Play!

Series Editor: Sandy Green

Guaranteed fun for children and practitioners alike, the Ready, Steady, Play! series provides lively and stimulating activities for children.

Each book focuses on one specific aspect of play offering clear and detailed guidance on how to plan and enjoy wonderful play experiences with minimum fuss and maximum success.

Each book in the Ready, Steady, Play! series includes advice on:

- How to prepare the children and the play space
- What equipment and materials are needed
- How much time is needed to prepare and carry out the activity
- How many staff are required
- How to communicate with parents and colleagues

Ready, Steady, Play! helps you to:

- Develop activities easily, using suggested guidelines
- Ensure that health and safety issues are taken into account
- Plan play that links to the early years curriculum
- Broaden your understanding of early years issues

Early years practitioners and students on early years courses and parents looking for simple, excellent ideas for creative play will love these books!

## Other titles in the series

Books, Stories and Puppets 1-84312-148-4 Green
Construction 1-84312-098-4 Boyd
Creativity 1-84312-076-3 Green
Displays and Interest Tables 1-84312-267-7 Olpin
Festivals 1-84312-101-8 Hewitson
Food and Cooking 1-84312-100-X Green
Nature, Living and Growing 1-84312-114-X Harper
Play Using Natural Materials 1-84312-099-2 Howe
Role Play 1-84312-147-6 Green

# Music and Singing

## Julie Durno

 David Fulton Publishers

David Fulton Publishers Ltd
The Chiswick Centre, 414 Chiswick High Road, London W4 5TF

www.fultonpublishers.co.uk

First published in Great Britain in 2006 by David Fulton Publishers

10 9 8 7 6 5 4 3 2 1

Note: The right of Julie Durno to be identified as the author of this work has been asserted by her in accordance with the Copyright, Designs and Patents Act 1988.

David Fulton Publishers is a division of Granada Learning Ltd, part of ITV plc.

*British Library Cataloguing in Publication Data*
A catalogue record for this book is available from the British Library.

ISBN 1-84312-276-6

Illustrations by Bethan Matthews (pp. 22, 28, 30, 34, 40, 48, 50, 51, 53, 60)
Typeset by FiSH Books, London
Printed and bound in Great Britain

# Contents

# Music and Singing

Welcome to *Music and Singing*, part of the exciting Ready, Steady, Play! series.

Get ready to enjoy a range of activities with your children, which will stimulate their all-round development.

The Ready, Steady, Play! books will help boost the confidence of new practitioners by providing information and fun ideas to support planning and preparation. The series will also consolidate and extend learning for the more experienced practitioner. Attention is drawn to health and safety, and the role of the adult is addressed.

## How to use this book

*Music and Singing* is divided into five main sections.

Section 1 reassures the reader that everyone can enjoy music with young children. Practitioners do not need to be able to play an instrument or to be a good singer, they simply need to be willing to get involved. This section also gives guidance on setting up the music area, and on buying, caring for and storing musical instruments.

The discussion resources in Section 2 provide a range of photographs of musical instruments and music making from around the world to stimulate discussion and enquiry.

Section 3 presents 18 activities, helping practitioners to introduce many different aspects of music to children to encourage aural discrimination, use of the senses and creativity.

The photocopiable pages in Section 4 support many of the activities with resources such as words to rhymes and songs.

Towards the end of the book readers will find music to accompany some of the activities and information on suppliers of useful resources and relevant websites.

So read on, and enjoy ... **Ready, Steady, Play!**

Sandy Green
Series editor

*To my Grandmother, Claire Casey,*
*who loved music and singing*

# Acknowledgements

I could not have written this book without the love and support of my husband Alastair. His interest, patience and total belief in me have been unwavering and I will always be grateful.

Thank you to my lovely daughters, Sophie and Sacha, for all the music and singing. Thanks are also due to Juliet Nicolaou from The Little Drum Music Group, Buckinghamshire, for providing me with support and inspiration. Long may we continue, partner! Thank you to Keith Hoffmeister for his encouragement and for taking so many of the photographs in this book. Thanks to Mrs Hillson of Ley Hill School for lending me her beautiful classroom. Thanks to Sue at Puppets by Post for providing exquisite puppets. Thanks to Margaret Marriott of David Fulton Publishers for being so obliging, calm and supportive. Thanks to Sandy Green for her professional expertise and guidance and friendly caring manner.

Grateful thanks to NES Arnold for permission to use photographs from their catalogue on pages 9–15 and 43.

And last but by no means least, thank you to Carole Carney for the pints of Earl Grey tea and for supporting me more than words can say.

## Series acknowledgement

The series editor would like to thank the children, parents and staff at:

- The Nursery and Reception classes, Wadebridge County Primary School, Wadebridge, Cornwall
- Happy Days Day Nursery, Wadebridge, Cornwall
- Snapdragons Nursery, Weston, Bath, Somerset
- Snapdragons Nursery, Grosvenor, Bath, Somerset
- Tadpoles Nursery, Combe Down, Bath, Somerset

for allowing us to take photographs of their excellent provision, resources and displays.

Also to John and Jake Green, Jasmine and Eva for their help throughout the series, and to Nina, Margaret and Ben at David Fulton Publishers for their patience, enthusiasm and support.

# Introduction

This practically led book has been written for Early Years students, practitioners and parents, to provide creative ideas for enjoying music and singing with young children.

Music forms a natural part of each human being and few children can resist including music in their lives, from swaying or tapping along to music to singing songs in the playground or humming along to a popular tune on the car radio.

You do not have to play an instrument or read music to teach music to very young children, and do not forget that children of this age are non-judgemental towards their teachers and carers.

It is not uncommon for people to quickly consider themselves as 'no good at music' or 'hopeless at singing', but enthusiasm, commitment and careful planning should result in music-making sessions that are full of fun and laughter, banishing feelings of inadequacy and building confidence.

## Why include music in the Early Years Curriculum?

Creativity is an important part of the Early Years Curriculum, and music making falls into this category.

Music making involves singing, dancing, composing, playing, movement and listening, and a carefully planned music session or activity may provide a child with opportunities to develop a number of competencies, skills and concepts across several areas of learning.

Here are some examples of how music can benefit children in each of the six areas of the Foundation Stage Curriculum:

**Personal, social and emotional development:** enjoying music from different cultures; talking about their own backgrounds; developing listening skills through listening to music; playing instruments encourages the children to wait their turn; playing in pairs or groups encourages team work; feelings can be explored and preferences expressed.

**Communication, language and literacy:** enjoying learning songs; changing the words to popular songs; acting out songs as stories; working in groups or pairs giving and taking instruction; expressing feelings and preferences through music appreciation; memorising names of instruments and how to play them; sounds and instruments can be compared and contrasted; sustaining attentive listening; extending vocabulary as new terms are introduced.

**Mathematical development:** reinforcing the recognised link between the learning of music and the understanding of mathematical concepts, e.g. counting songs; recognising patterns; exploring rhythm and beat and comparisons such as higher/lower, faster/slower; talking about shapes and using size language.

**Knowledge and understanding of the world:** exploring past and present; singing lullabies from babyhood; gaining awareness of other cultures through singing songs and playing music and instruments from around the world; learning how to operate musical equipment; using all of their senses.

**Physical development:** moving to music; freely expressing themselves; repeating a range of movements; copying physical actions; having an awareness of space when moving to music; hand–eye coordination when playing instruments; improving manipulative dexterity.

**Creative development:** combining different media when making and then playing instruments; recognising repeated sounds; matching movements to music; singing songs from memory; tapping out simple rhythms; making up dances; choosing paint colours to symbolise emotions; exploring how sounds can be changed; matching sounds to instruments and making comparisons.

## Points to remember

■ Warm up at the start of music sessions to relax adults and children! Try singing a familiar song or listening to a short piece of favourite music.

- Include music at some point every day. It is such an important part of our culture and should not be confined to music sessions only.

- Try replacing story time with music time occasionally, listening to a piece of music or singing songs. Involve the children in their selection.

- Gentle background music can work well when you are trying to calm children and set the scene. Try playing music at tidy-up time or when the children are having their snack. Vary the tempo for the mood that you wish to create (see examples on pages 71–3).

- Many genuine, positive comments in highly supportive surroundings are needed to make each child feel valued, relaxed and confident. Be specific in your praise, such as 'Well done, you stopped playing exactly when the music did' or 'I liked the sound you made when you tapped the claves, it sounded like footsteps'.

- Give the children a chance to voice their preferences and feelings, for example 'Which sound do you like the most, the shakers or the rainstick?' or 'Do you like this music? Does it make you feel happy or sad?' or 'What does this sound remind you of?'

- Provide music from as many sources as possible (see pages 71–3 for suggestions) and encourage the children to choose and to operate the music player if appropriate. Try to broaden the experiences of each child. Remember that it may be their first taste of a variety of music.

- Music and singing make a most successful outdoor activity. Find a shady spot and sit the children on a rug and encourage them to listen carefully and identify 'music' in the sounds around them (rustling leaves, birdsong, distant hum of traffic, clickety clack of train track, water sounds, wind, etc.).

- Continue with singing, playing instruments or using the activities that lend themselves to outdoors.

- Always thank the children for their contribution and clap each other at the end of playing and at the session end. Always reward solo and group playing with warm praise and applause.

- Enlist help! Is there a carer or sibling who would come and play an instrument to the children? Ask the local school if the orchestra would like to come and play and show their instruments to the children, or perhaps there is a local band or choir? Perhaps the older children could visit a recording studio or radio station? Would any grandparents like to come and sing some songs from their childhood or school days? (See Activity 4 on pages 26–7.)

## Instruments

It is worth buying the best instruments that you can afford from a reputable supplier (try NES Arnold or similar). Inferior instruments tend to break easily and may be dangerous, having sharp edges and spilling bead contents if played vigorously.

Instruments from around the world will add variety and will be of great interest to the children; however, bear in mind that they may not be as robust or safe as commercially produced items. Supervise their use carefully.

Try to build up a selection of different sounding instruments. The most common types of instruments used in the classroom are percussion instruments.

Percussion instruments fall into two categories: tuned (such as glockenspiels and chime bars) and untuned (such as a tambourine or triangle) where the notes played cannot be changed. Try to include both in your selection.

The most popular classroom percussion instruments are listed below.

### Metal

Sleigh bells
Triangle
Cymbals
Jingle (bell) stick
Tambourine
Chime bars
Xylophone
Handled bells
Hand bells

### Wood

Claves
Woodblocks
Castanets

Tulip block
Guiro
Wooden maracas
Wooden clackers

### Skin

Tambour
Tambourine
Drums (include a
selection to produce
different sounds)

### Hollow

Maracas
Rainsticks
Shakers
Guiros
Tulip block

### Tuned

Glockenspiel
Chime bars
Xylophone
Metallophone

## Care of instruments

Instruments should be stored out of direct sunlight and away from heat sources. A trolley is ideal, with instruments stored in clear boxes for easy access.

Show the children how to play each instrument correctly and safely at the start of each session and always use the correct name for the instruments. Let them experiment by using different beaters to create different sounds and show them that incorrect playing will alter or spoil the sound.

Always involve the children in putting the instruments away neatly and they will become familiar and confident with them. Wipe instruments over with a damp cloth and dry to keep them clean. Do not immerse them in water.

## Useful hand signals

Show the children a simple set of hand signals that will be used in future music sessions. Ensure that all practitioners use the same signals to avoid confusion. The children will soon become familiar with them.

Familiar hand signals encourage the children to watch the practitioner closely thus improving their concentration levels. They enable adjustment of volume levels and maintainence of control without raising voices above the noise or interrupting the flow of music making.

You may wish to try these examples:

*Quiet*

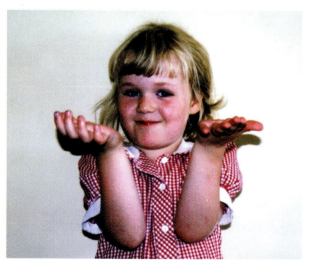

*Louder*

*Stop*

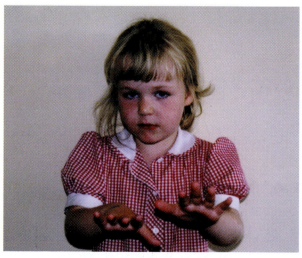

*Quieter*

## The music area

If space is at a premium, use a trolley or similar as a music area, the benefit being that it can be moved around, inside and out. Instruments can be stored in clear lidded boxes for easy recognition, with the correct beaters stored in the same box.

Some practitioners feel that the music area works best if it is set up for a short period and then removed so that the children are more inspired to use it when it appears! Others feel that the area is a valuable asset to the classroom and if space allows, it should be left out for the children to use as the mood takes them. See which method suits your setting.

Both children and practitioners need to be comfortable when enjoying the music area. You may wish to carpet the floor or provide soft cushions, bean bags or small chairs. Carpet or cork tiles on the walls, floors and shelves will absorb some sound and protect the instruments if they are on open shelving.

Encourage all the children to work in the area in pairs or small groups. You may wish to ask them to post their names in a box when they have used it so that you can keep a record.

## The adult role

The adult plays an important part during successful music sessions in the following ways:

- Planning activities carefully and providing the necessary equipment and prepared areas.
- Giving specific praise and encouragement to all children.
- Observing the children and recording their progress.
- Linking music sessions to other class topics and providing extension activities where appropriate.
- Encouraging language development through discussion and unhurried, open questioning.
- Ensuring that the activities are suitable for the stage of development of the group.

- Ensuring that each child makes a contribution to the session and is made to feel valued, relaxed and unthreatened.
- Your enthusiasm, commitment and professional judgement can create an exciting world of music. Have fun!

## Health and safety

Throughout this book, there are reminders about health and safety which are summarised below:

- Ensure adequate space for movement.
- Remind children how to play instruments safely and correctly at the beginning of each session.
- During creative work, take care when using scissors, glue, paints, bodkins, etc. and always work in a protected area.
- Paints, glue, colouring pens/pencils/crayons, etc. must be safe for young children.
- Small items such as beads, grains, sequins, pebbles, etc. must not be placed in mouths, noses or ears.
- Clear up spills immediately and thoroughly to prevent slipping.
- Supervise use of electrical equipment very carefully, reminding children that an adult must be present at all times.
- Lengths of ribbon, string, braid and elastic can be hazardous and should be used with care.
- Cling film boxes have a serrated edge and film must not be put near faces.
- Stand bottles in a secure place such as a plant trough.
- Containers must be clean, smooth edged and dry before using.
- Care must be taken when using glass bottles. Do not strike them too hard.

Remember, music should be fun and educational. As Plato said:

Music gives a soul to the universe, wings to the mind, flight to the imagination, and life to everything.

# Discussion resources

The following section provides a range of photographs and pictures to stimulate discussion with children, broadening their knowledge of musical instruments.

Percussion instruments

Chime bars and xylophones

Konga

Djembe

Floor tom

Tubano

Bongos

Ocean drums

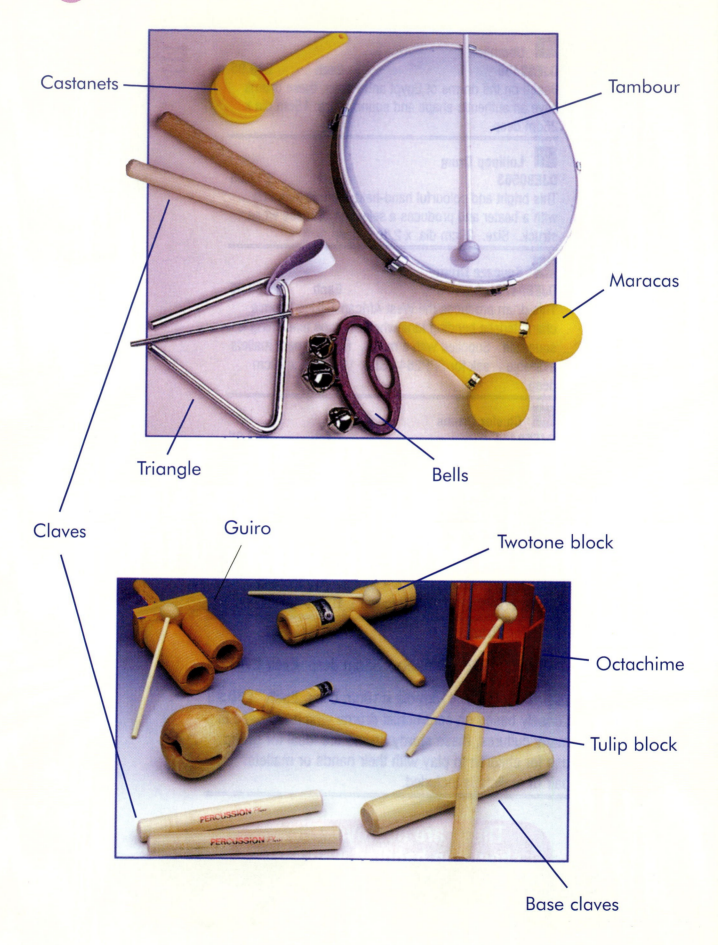

Castanets

Tambour

Maracas

Triangle

Bells

Claves

Guiro

Twotone block

Octachime

Tulip block

Base claves

Percussion instruments

Playbells

Hand bells

Guiros

Handled maracas

Star tambourines

Steel drum

Wrist and ankle bells

Clatter-pillar

Rhythm instruments

First drum

Concertina

Brass band

Orchestra

Violin

Guitar

Double bass

Cello

Viola

Harp

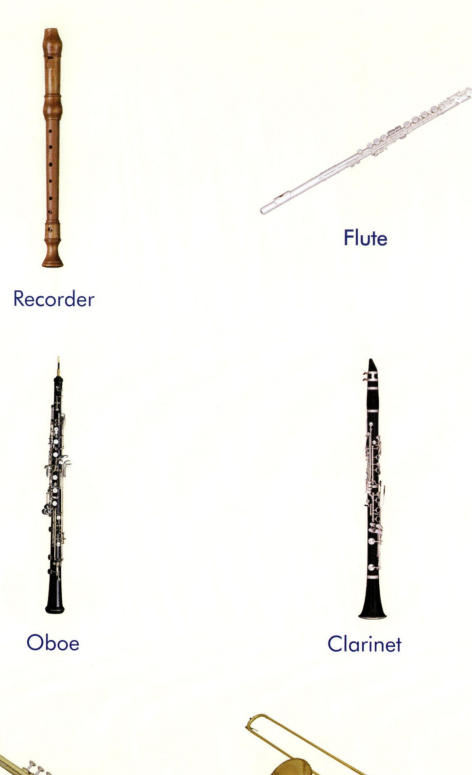

Recorder

Flute

Oboe

Clarinet

Trumpet

Trombone

# Activities

The following pages contain 18 different activities relating to music and singing. Each activity follows a standard format to ensure ease of planning and implementation:

- the resources needed
- the aim(s)/concept(s)
- the process
- group size
- health and safety
- vocabulary discussion
- extension ideas
- links to the Foundation Stage Curriculum.

## Key to Foundation Stage Curriculum abbreviations:

**SS**    Stepping stones

**ELG**    Early learning goals

**PSE**    Personal, social and emotional development

**CLL**    Communication, language and literacy

**MD**    Mathematical development

**KUW**    Knowledge and understanding of the world

**PD**    Physical development

**CD**    Creative development

# ACTIVITY 1

# Singing and sequencing

## Resources you will need

### Part A

- Large plastic hoop

### Part B

- Old Lady puppet (optional; see photocopiable sheet 1 on page 58)
- Animals to be fed to her (these could be small world animals, pictures or finger puppets)

## Aim/concept

- To encourage imagination and develop recall

## Process

- (Parts A and B) Explain to children what the activity is about.
- Sing the song 'There Was an Old Lady' to the children, encouraging them to listen carefully. (See photocopiable sheet 2 on page 59 for words.)
- Discuss the song: ask if they liked it, what did they like about it, and ask if they have heard it before.

### Part A

- Divide the group into categories, i.e. fly, spider, bird, cat, etc.
- Ask each group to move carefully like their creature, making appropriate sounds.
- Hold the hoop upright resting on the floor (this becomes the Old Lady's mouth).
- While singing the song again with the children, ask them to move into the mouth as their creature is mentioned.
- Children who have been 'swallowed' sit on the other side of the hoop making munching sounds as the others are eaten.
- Ask the children to recall and recount the sequence.
- Interchange the children into different categories.

### Part B

- Introduce the Old Lady puppet to the children (instructions on how to make her are on photocopiable sheet 1 on page 58).
- The Old Lady tells the children about the largest meal she ever ate!

- Sing the song with the group (see photocopiable sheet 2 on page 59), feeding the creatures into her mouth as appropriate. Place the animals out of view as they are swallowed.
- Ask the children to recall and recount the sequence.
- Sing the song again and, if appropriate, allow the children to feed the Old Lady.

## Vocabulary/discussion

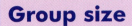

- Discuss animal sounds and movements, e.g. buzzing, flying, creeping
- Use comparative language: similar to, smaller than, larger than, etc.
- (Part A) Use positional language: in, out, behind, through, following
- Talk about body parts and sounds relating to them: mouth, throat, tummy, swallowing, eating, chewing, crunching

## Group size

Whole group

## Extension ideas

1. Small groups to make Old Lady puppet to use during the song.
2. Make the creatures to be swallowed using felt, fabric or card.
3. Explore other sequencing songs in the same way, e.g. 'Old Macdonald' (traditional words and tune).
4. Sing other songs about food and eating, e.g. 'Naan Bread in the Oven' (see photocopiable sheet 3 on page 60).
5. Sing the 'There Was an Old Lady' song again, making up new words with the children, e.g. introducing new creatures.

## Links to Foundation Stage Curriculum

**SS** Move freely with pleasure and confidence (PD)

**ELG** Move with confidence, imagination and in safety (PD)

**SS** Respond to sound with body movement (CD)

**SS** Join in favourite songs (CD)

**SS** **ELG** Recognise and explore how sounds can be changed, sing simple songs from memory, recognise repeated sounds and sound patterns and match movements to music (CD)

## Health and safety

⚠ Careful supervision of small items
⚠ Ensure safe space for movement for size of group
⚠ Discuss with the children the importance of not putting unsuitable items in their mouths
⚠ (Part B) Careful supervision of scissors, needle and wool, small eye stickers, etc.

# ACTIVITY 2 Musical mood pictures

## Resources you will need

- Music player and a selection of music tapes/CDs to evoke different moods (see pages 71 for suggestions)
- Protected painting area, painting overalls
- Wide range of coloured paints to include light and dark colours
- Fat and thin paintbrushes
- Sheets of A3/A2 paper (write the heading 'Listening to Vivaldi made Lily feel...' and leave a space for a mood sticker, folding this section back to keep it unpainted)
- Face shapes or stickers showing a range of emotions, e.g. happy, sad, sleepy (see photocopiable sheet 4 on page 61)

## Aim/concept

- To help children to express their feelings through painting while listening to music

## Process

- Explain to the children that they are going to be listening to different pieces of music and at the same time, painting to show how the music makes them feel.
- Ask them if they like listening to music and ask when and where they enjoy it, what their favourite music is, etc.
- Explain how music can be used to create atmosphere.
- Play short pieces to the group which create different moods, encouraging the children to listen carefully. Use approximately three contrasting pieces of music (see page 71 for suggestions).
- Ask the children how each piece made them feel and whether they enjoyed each one.
- Replay the first piece and encourage the group to begin painting, allowing their mood to help them select colours and style of painting (encourage abstract painting if possible).
- Each time ask children to select a face from the shapes or stickers provided which illustrates their feelings and stick it to the top of their painting next to their name. Alternatively, a set of six emotions hand puppets from NES Arnold could be used (see 'Resources' on page 74).
- Repeat with the next piece of music.

## Vocabulary/discussion

- Explore emotive language: happy, sad, frightened, sleepy, playful, energetic, relaxed
- Describe music (e.g. loud, quiet, peaceful, fast, slow, modern, classical, pop, TV, film) and discuss its origins
- Describe where each piece originates: Irish folk music, Indian music, Scottish bagpipes, African drums, etc.
- Consider likes and dislikes
- Encourage and introduce language used to describe the pictures: light, pale, bright, swirls, twists, spots, dark, jagged, gloomy, shady, sunny, wintery, zigzag, etc.

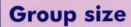

Listening to Vivaldi made Lily feel ☺

## Group size

4–6

## Extension ideas

1. Study finished paintings when dry. Compare them, asking the children what they like about each other's. Did the music evoke similar feelings?
2. Children help to sort pictures and plan a display.
3. Listen to the pieces again on a different day. Do they make the children feel the same?
4. Repeat the activity using different mood music and art materials.
5. Listen to one piece of music and make a collage as a group (e.g. listening to reggae might lead to a summer holiday collage).
6. Use music in movement sessions to encourage physical expression.

## Links to Foundation Stage Curriculum

**SS** Notice and comment on patterns (KUW)

**ELG** Look closely at similarities, differences, patterns and change. Ask questions about why things happen and how things work (KUW)

**SS** Show an interest in what they see, hear, smell, touch and feel (CD)

**ELG** Express and communicate their ideas, thoughts and feelings by using a widening range of materials, suitable tools, imaginative and role play, movement, designing and making and a variety of songs and musical instruments (CD)

## Health and safety

⚠ Ensure that children are well covered
⚠ Supervise carefully, clearing up spills immediately
⚠ Wash hands thoroughly at the end of the activity
⚠ Use non-toxic paint

# Join our orchestra

## Resources you will need

- Discussion resource (pages 9–18)
- Photographs of orchestras or bands
- Tape/CD player with orchestral/brass/steel band music to listen to
- Groups of instruments for the children to play laid out on a table (e.g. bells, shakers, drums, claves, cymbals, castanets, tambourines)
- Camera if required

## Aim/concept

- To show the children that many different instruments can play together to produce a piece of music

## Process

- Show the children pictures of orchestras and/or bands and discuss where they may be seen. Have the children ever seen them, and if so, where?
- Discuss which instruments they can see in the pictures.
- Explain how they are going to create their own orchestra.
- Ask them to listen carefully to two pieces of chosen music.
- Ask the children to identify any individual instrument sounds, replaying the music if necessary.
- Encourage them to select an instrument and to sit in groups according to instruments chosen.
- Remind the children of the hand signals shown on page 6 and encourage them to play along to a simple song, e.g. 'Twinkle, Twinkle Little Star'.
- Repeat using hand signals to alter volume etc. and repeat allowing one type of instrument to play each line.
- Encourage the children to take turns to role play the conductor using hand signals as shown.
- Change instruments and vary songs as appropriate.
- Take photographs for display if required.

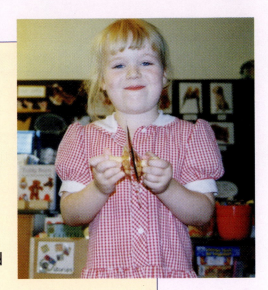

## Vocabulary/discussion

- Define words such as orchestra, band, musician, performer
- Encourage children to name as many instruments as possible (e.g. trumpets, drums, piano, violins, etc.), including the percussion instruments on the table
- Talk about music in terms of loud, quiet, fast, slow, happy, sad
- Discuss likes and dislikes of pre-recorded pieces, songs and sounds created

## Group size

Whole group

## Extension ideas

1. Discuss instrument groupings in an orchestra, e.g. woodwind, brass, string, percussion, showing examples if possible.
2. Make a display with the heading 'Welcome to our orchestra' surrounded by paintings/drawings and photographs of the children playing their instruments.
3. Leave the instruments on display in their groupings to encourage future group playing.

## Links to Foundation Stage Curriculum

**SS** Listen to favourite nursery rhymes, stories and songs. Join in with repeated refrains, anticipating key events and important phrases (CLL)

**ELG** Sustain attentive listening, responding to what they have heard by relevant comments, questions or actions (CLL)

**SS** Show an interest in the way musical instruments sound (CD)

**SS** Explore the different sounds of instruments (CD)

**ELG** Recognise and explore how sounds can be changed, sing simple songs from memory, recognise repeated sounds and sound patterns and match movements to music (CD)

## Health and safety

⚠ Remind the children how to use the instruments safely, e.g. do not put in mouth or play too close to faces

## ACTIVITY 4 Lullaby time

### Resources you will need

- Music player
- CDs or tapes with lullabies, baby songs, etc.
- Childrens' favourite baby songs as suggested by their parents and carers
- Favourite teddies or dolls from home or a selection provided by Nursery
- A photograph of the children as babies, put into a small album beforehand if possible
- Soft drawstring bag or pillowcase to hold the soft toys
- A camera (optional)

### Aim/concept

- For the children to learn simple lullabies, while sharing experiences of their past

### Process

- Introduce the children to your favourite childhood toy, explaining why it is special to you.
- Take a toy out of the bag and encourage the children to guess its name and who it belongs to. Repeat until everyone has their toy (explain that some toys are too precious to be brought in and allow those without a toy to choose from your selection).
- Ask the children to say a little about their toy and talk about why they like it. Does it smell/feel nice? Does it feel soft/rough/furry/silky?
- What does it remind them of? Who bought it for them? How old is it? Where does it live? Are any of them similar?
- Borrowed toys can be discussed in a similar way: why did they choose it? What makes it special? How does it look and feel?
- Sitting in a circle, tell the children about some of the rhymes and songs that their parents have told you about. Ask if they can remember them.
- Encourage the children to sing some of the special baby songs to their teddy or doll, with or without music (examples can be found on photocopiable sheet 5 on page 62).
- Pass the baby photographs round and discuss them, encouraging the children to talk about their memories, feelings and experiences.
- Explain what a lullaby is and finish the activity singing an easy lullaby to their toy.

## Vocabulary/discussion

- Encourage the children to describe their favourite teddy/toy, e.g. furry, rough, silky, soft, cuddly, comforting, familiar, favourite, etc.
- Introduce words to describe their babyhood, e.g. newborn, parents, grandparents, relatives, crying, feeding, sleeping, cuddly, tiny. Explore physical characteristics and cultural identity
- Use vocabulary linked to lullabies: soothing, calming, peaceful, sleepy, dreamy, night-time, etc.

## Group size

4–8

## Extension ideas

1. Link the activity to a theme on 'ourselves' and/or our families.
2. Create a display showing their baby photographs and photographs taken of them singing to their toy babies. Include drawings or paintings of themselves as babies and/or as they look now.
3. Finish each session with a lullaby, allowing the children to choose their favourites.
4. Ask some parents/carers to come in and sing baby songs or lullabies from their childhoods and varying cultures.
5. Children could perform their lullabies to their parents and carers.
6. Practitioners can share their toys, photographs and experiences with the children.

## Links to Foundation Stage Curriculum

**SS** Talk freely about their home and community (PSE)

**SS** Have a sense of self as a member of different communities (PSE)

**ELG** Have a developing awareness of their own needs, views and feelings and be sensitive to the needs, views and feelings of others. Have a developing respect for their own cultures and beliefs and those of other people (PSE)

**SS** Begin to differentiate between past and present (KUW)

**ELG** Find out about past and present events in their own lives, and in those of their families and other people they know (KUW)

## Health and safety

⚠ No specific issues to be taken into consideration

## ACTIVITY 5 Counting songs

### Resources you will need

- Aprons
- 10 small, empty plastic green bottles with lids
- 10 pieces of string approximately 50 cm long
- 10 pieces of Blu-tack
- Sticky tape
- A drum or tambourine
- A recording of 'Ten Green Bottles' (optional; see 'Resources' on page 72)
- Music player

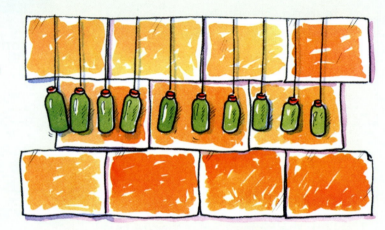

### Aim/concept

- To act out a familiar counting song, involving the children in its preparation and encouraging careful listening

### Process

- In advance, provide an opportunity for the children to create A4-sized bricks to make a wall, attach them to a large sheet of paper.
- Remind the children of the brick wall that they made previously. Discuss how well they have worked on it.
- Using sticky tape, attach the completed wall to a table edge or chest of drawers and hang the bottles in front of the wall using Blu-tack attached to the table or drawer surface.
- Count the bottles as a group. Try counting backwards depending on the stage of the children's development.
- Sing 'Ten Green Bottles' (traditional words and tune), allowing each child to pull one bottle to the floor on the word 'fall'.
- You may wish to bang a drum or tambourine on the word 'fall' and invite the children to clap, encouraging careful listening.
- Allow children to re-hang bottles and repeat. Fewer bottles may be used according to group size and age.
- Display on the wall if possible.

## Vocabulary/discussion

- Introduce terms such as rough, smooth, square, oblong, rectangle, pattern, texture, shape, rows and layers to describe the bricks
- Count up to 10 bottles, counting forwards and backwards using fingers to help
- Discuss brick wall patterns, shapes and colours and textures with the children
- Use positional language for the wall: in front of, behind, on top of, above, next to, beside

## Group size

Up to ten

## Extension ideas

1. Sing other counting songs, e.g. '1, 2, 3, 4, 5 Once I Caught a Fish Alive, (song words are shown on photocopiable sheets 6 and 7). Children could make or use a fish to bite their finger.
2. Act out 'Five Currant Buns in a Baker's Shop' using play food, money, etc.
3. Sing 'Ten Fat Sausages Sizzling in a Pan' to the tune of 'Ten Green Bottles'. Use drums or tambourines to 'pop' the sausages and play food sausages in a pan to aid counting.
4. Sing other counting songs, e.g. 'This Old Man', 'The Ants Went Marching', 'Ten Little Toys', 'Five Little Leaves', etc. Note: there are puppets available from Puppets By Post (see 'Resources' on page 72) which can be used to bring many of the counting songs to life.

## Links to Foundation Stage Curriculum

**SS** Enjoy joining in with number rhymes and songs (MD)

**SS** Say the number after any number up to 9 (MD)

**ELG** Say and use number names in order in familiar contexts (MD)

**ELG** Count reliably up to 10 everyday objects (MD)

**ELG** Recognise numerals 1 to 9 (MD)

**SS** Work creatively on a large or small scale (CD)

**ELG** Explore colour, texture, shape, form and space in two or three dimensions (CD)

## Health and safety

⚠ Be careful when using lengths of string
⚠ Ensure that the children do not place bottle tops in their mouths

**ACTIVITY 6**

# Make a shaker

## Resources you will need

- A selection of matching clean, dry pots with lids (opaque plastic, if possible)
- Screw-topped, clean heavy-duty glass jars and tins
- A variety of substances such as lentils, dried peas, rice, sand, pasta shapes, small stones
- Sticky tape
- Sticky labels
- Cling film
- Elastic bands
- Music player and selection of favourite songs (optional)

## Aim/concept

- To make a variety of different shakers to be used as percussion instruments

## Process

- If possible, show the children a range of shakers and maracas and ask them to guess what is inside.
- Ask if they like the sounds, what are the sounds similar to, which is their favourite, etc.
- Explain that they are going to make their own shakers and stress the importance of not putting the substances into their mouth, nose or ears!
- Encourage the children to work in pairs, taking a container and adding one type of substance until it is 1/3rd full. Organise them so that there are two matching pots of each substance.
- Securely fasten the lid with sticky tape and help each child to number their pot with a sticky label. Place in number order to one side.
- Ask the children to identify the contents of the numbered pots. Which ones are the same?
- Encourage the children to experiment with different sized pots and jars to produce a range of shakers.
- As a group, explore the sounds made by the various substances in the matching pots. Display in similar sounding pairs.
- Play or sing some favourite songs using the shakers as percussion instruments.
- Label each shaker with the child's name and display on the music table.

## Vocabulary/discussion

- Introduce new vocabulary to describe sounds, e.g. loud/soft, nice/nasty, rough/gentle, fast/slow, crackling, swishing, hollow, tinkling, rattling
- What do the sounds remind them of? The sea, the wind, breaking glass, heavy rain, crunchy snow, sweets in a jar?
- Use comparative language: largest/smallest, loudest/quietest, the same, similar

## Group size

Whole group

## Extension ideas

1. Build up a sequence of shaker sounds related to a story or visit to a familiar place, e.g. the seaside, or going on a train journey.
2. Encourage the children to make their own suggestions, e.g. snow falling, ice crunching, wind blowing, snowball hitting a coat, etc.
3. Divide the group into two and see which group can identify the shaker contents most accurately.
4. Hold up picture cards (e.g. large and small animals, different weather, birds, insects) and ask the children to choose which shaker best represents it.
5. Decide with the children which weather is represented by which shaker, and then play them behind a screen to see if they can identify the sounds.

## Links to Foundation Stage Curriculum

**SS** Have a positive approach to new experiences (PSE)

**SS** Show confidence in linking up with others for support and guidance (PSE)

**ELG** Continue to be interested, excited and motivated to learn (PSE)

**ELG** Be confident to try new activities, initiate ideas and speak in a familiar group (PSE)

**SS** Respond to comments and questions, entering into dialogue about their creations (CD)

**SS** Make comparisons (CD)

**ELG** Express and communicate their ideas, thoughts and feelings by using a widening range of materials, suitable tools, imaginative and role play, movement, designing and making, and a variety of songs and musical instruments (CD)

## Health and safety

- ⚠ Stress the importance of not placing the shaker contents in their mouth, nose or ears
- ⚠ Containers must be clean, dry and smooth edged
- ⚠ Ensure that lids or film tops are securely fastened before playing
- ⚠ Cling film can be dangerous and box edge is serrated
- ⚠ Careful supervision is needed if using glass jars

# What's in the bag?

## Resources you will need

- Large drawstring bag or pillowcase
- A selection of instruments

## Aim/concept

- To develop the children's listening skills by identifying a variety of percussion instruments through touch and sound only

## Process

- Ask the children to sit down and discuss how important listening is (see 'Vocabulary/discussion' opposite).
- To encourage careful listening, ask the children to close their eyes and move among them playing an instrument (e.g. a triangle), asking them to point to where the sound is coming from.
- Experiment playing up high, down low, loudly and softly, moving the sound as much as possible. Have fun with other practitioners using different instruments.
- Without the children seeing, place an instrument in the bag and ask them to come forward in pairs to feel the bag and try to guess the instrument inside (see 'Vocabulary/discussion' opposite).
- Open the bag and place your hands inside to play the instrument, encouraging careful listening.
- Is the sound high/low, loud/quiet, familiar/unfamiliar, pleasant/unpleasant?
- Can they guess the instrument correctly? Ask them to repeat the correct name of the instrument.
- Allow them to play it, if appropriate, and repeat.

## Vocabulary/discussion

- Discuss the importance of listening, e.g. to hear instructions, warnings, to learn, to enjoy conversation, music, television and cinema, to hear stories, to learn language, etc.
- Describe instruments – hard/soft, loud/quiet, large/small, round/square/triangular, familiar/unfamiliar, pleasant/unpleasant
- Use comparative language to describe instruments: a triangle is shaped like a roof, shakers look like bottles, a tambourine is shaped like a wheel

## Group size

Flexible

## Extension ideas

1. Play Chinese whispers in a circle to encourage careful listening and have some fun with the outcomes!
2. In a small group, each child is given an instrument in a drawstring bag or pillowcase and asked to feel and guess what it is. The children then all play along to a simple, familiar song.

## Links to Foundation Stage Curriculum

| | |
|---|---|
| SS | Show curiosity (PSE) |
| SS | Have a strong exploratory impulse (PSE) |
| ELG | Maintain attention, concentrate and sit quietly when appropriate (PSE) |
| SS | Use size language such as big and little (MD) |
| SS | Begin to talk about the shapes of everyday objects (MD) |
| ELG | Use language such as 'greater', 'smaller', 'heavier', or 'lighter' to compare quantities (MD) |
| SS | Show curiosity, observe and manipulate objects (KUW) |
| ELG | Investigate objects and materials by using all of their senses as appropriate (KUW) |

## Health and safety

⚠ Remind the children how to play instruments safely
⚠ Be aware of any sharp edges, points, etc. when instruments are in the bag

# ACTIVITY 8 Make a water xylophone

## Resources you will need

- Six glass bottles of the same size and shape
- Water to pour into the bottles
- Food dye, ink or paint to colour the water
- Different textured beaters, e.g. wooden spoon, metal ruler, rubber-ended beater, plastic-ended beater, a pencil, a fork, etc.
- Coloured discs of card the same colours as the water
- Cling film and elastic bands to cover tops if necessary
- A plastic funnel

## Aim/concept

- To introduce notation

## Process

- Explain to the children that they are going to make a water xylophone.
- Take them to a prepared, protected area and help them to pour coloured water into the bottles to varying levels.
- Stand bottles in a light-weight plant trough for safety and stability.
- Show the children how to play the xylophone with various beaters producing different sounds.
- Arrange the bottles from high to low and see if they can play any abstract tunes of their own.
- If you can, play the first few notes of a familiar song (e.g. 'Twinkle, Twinkle Little Star').
- Help the children to play the tune if possible.
- See if they are able to play their own made-up tunes. Ask them which sounds they like best and why.
- Have fun playing different notes with different beaters and moving the bottles into different orders. Ask the children to suggest different beaters.
- The water xylophone can be left on display for children to explore in their own time.

## Vocabulary/discussion

- Talk about making the xylophone: pouring, dye, ink, colours, full, empty, equal, level, beater materials, wood, metal, glass, plastic, rubber
- Use comparative language: higher than, lower than, the same as, quieter than, louder than, similar to
- Explain that music is written in notes and introduce the word note(s) during the activity
- Use the terms high, low, loud, quiet, soft, etc.

## Group size

4–6

## Extension ideas

1. Use different types of bottles, larger, smaller, plastic, etc., to create different sounds.
2. Show the children a wooden xylophone and let them play it. Explore differences and similarities between the two types of xylophone.
3. Help the children to notate their own pieces using coloured discs. These could form part of a display.
4. Show the children some simple music and explain that it is used in the same way as books are read.

## Links to Foundation Stage Curriculum

| | |
|---|---|
| **SS** | Show increasing independence in selecting and carrying out activities (PSE) |
| **ELG** | Be confident in trying out new activities, initiating ideas and speaking in a familiar group (PSE) |
| **SS** | Talk about what is seen and what is happening (KUW) |
| **ELG** | Ask questions about why things happen and how things work (KUW) |

## Health and safety

- ⚠ Work in a protected area and wipe up spills immediately
- ⚠ Children who are sensitive to dyes should wear protective gloves
- ⚠ Remind the children not to drink any of the liquids
- ⚠ Supervise the activity closely and do not allow the children to strike glass bottles too hard
- ⚠ Assist the children when using cling film as it must not be placed over mouth and nose, and the box edge is serrated
- ⚠ Stand bottles in a secure place such as a plant trough

**ACTIVITY 9**

# Make a recording

## Resources you will need

- A basic tape recorder, battery operated if possible
- Blank cassettes and pre-recorded tapes (classical, contemporary, talking books, etc.)
- Thin card cut into cassette-box title covers (use the original card inserts as templates)
- Colouring pencils and crayons
- A range of percussion instruments
- Pictures and photographs of a recording studio for discussion

## Aim/concept

- To produce their own music tape, showing that music and sounds can be recorded, and to learn to operate a tape recorder

## Process

- Explain to the children that they are going to produce their own tape.
- Show them the tape recorder and explain how to operate it (rewinding, re-recording, etc. until they are happy with the sound).
- Help the children to choose a percussion instrument and discuss which of their favourite songs they would like to record.
- Begin the recording by introducing themselves and their instrument. Singing their name is fun too.
- When settled, ask one child to be the sound engineer and on his or her instruction, begin singing and playing along while being recorded. Use the hand signals as shown on page 6.
- When they are happy with the recording, choose another sound engineer and repeat the exercise to build up a tape of songs.
- Help the children to design a cassette-box cover using their own designs and label the boxes with their name.
- Store the cassettes carefully in a lidded shoebox in the music area, and encourage the children to listen to them during future sessions, discussing the differences, their favourites, etc.

## Vocabulary/discussion

- Describe the cassette player using words such as volume, up, down, rewind, fast forward, record, erase, pause
- Discuss the recording studio – sound engineer, knobs, switches, microphone, CDs, vinyl records, musicians, soundtracks, etc.
- Identify the correct names of percussion instruments
- Use comparative language: loudest/quietest, longest/shortest, most popular/least popular, etc.

## Group size

4

## Extension ideas

1. Make an activity book showing how the children created their own tapes. Use drawings, photos and paintings to illustrate it.
2. Make a cassette tape for each child to give as a gift to parents/carers, or as a Nursery fundraising activity.
3. Encourage the children to use the cassette recorder to record sounds indoors and outdoors. This could link to other topics and themes, e.g. weather or nature.
4. Make a 'listening walk tape' of sounds from around the setting and try and guess what each sound relates to (e.g. a door closing, the toilet flushing, water play, bricks falling).

## Links to Foundation Stage Curriculum

**SS** Use writing as a means of recording and communicating (CLL)

**ELG** Write their own names and other things such as labels and captions and begin to form simple sentences sometimes using punctuation (CLL)

**SS** Know how to operate simple equipment (KUW)

**ELG** Find out about and identify the uses of everyday technology and use information and communication technology... to support their learning (KUW)

**SS** Engage in activities requiring hand–eye coordination (PD)

**ELG** Handle tools, objects, construction and malleable materials safely and with increasing control (PD)

## Health and safety

⚠ Ensure that the tape-recording equipment is in good working order

⚠ Children must be reminded how to use electrical equipment correctly at the beginning of each session and be supervised at all times

⚠ Observe children closely while making the listening walk tape (shutting doors, flushing toilets, etc.) and keep to small groups if possible

## ACTIVITY 10   Travelling to nursery

### Resources you will need

- Chairs
- A selection of percussion instruments
- Ribbon sticks (see Activity 15)
- Books or photographs of modes of transport
- A recording of 'The Wheels on the Bus' song (see 'Resources' on page 72)
- Music player
- Hat, jacket, name badge, etc. for the driver (optional)

### Aim/concept

- To build a repertoire of songs that relate to everyday life

### Process

- Explain to the group that you are going to sing some songs about how we travel around.
- Using discussion resources, if available, ask the children how they travel to Nursery.
- Stimulate discussion about various modes of transport, both familiar and unfamiliar. Encourage comparisons, benefits, likes and dislikes.
- Help the children to set out their chairs in pairs, all facing the front to resemble the seating on a bus. Explain that you will soon give each child an instrument.
- Ask the children to listen to 'The Wheels on the Bus' song carefully and then ask them to decide which percussion instruments best match the actions in the song.
- Hand out the instruments and remind the children how to play correctly and safely, being considerate when changing seats.
- Play/sing the song again using percussion instruments (e.g. ribbon sticks for wipers, shakers for chattering, tambourines for babies shouting, triangles for the bell), changing roles and instruments from time to time.

## Vocabulary/discussion

- Talk about modes of transport, mentioning as many as possible and including some unusual methods (e.g. a rickshaw, pony and trap). Show pictures if possible
- Use comparative language to explore preferences, advantages and disadvantages, etc.
- Discuss sounds of percussion instruments, the correct names of each and how to use them correctly
- Memorise the words to 'The Wheels on the Bus' song

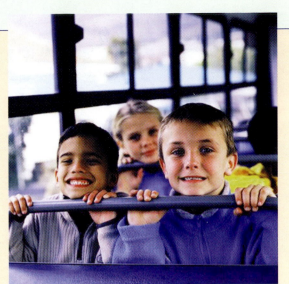

## Group size

Whole group or 4–6 : 1

## Extension ideas

1. Link to topics on travel, transport or the environment.
2. Sing other transport-related songs such as: 'My Bicycle Has a Bell', 'Down at the Station', 'I'm Driving in My Car', 'I Had a Little Engine', 'John Brown's Tractor', 'Trot, Trot, Trot', 'Row Your Boat', 'Ride a Cock Horse', 'The Big Ship Sails on the Alley, Alley O' (see 'Resources' on page 72).
3. Link to a topic on road safety. Contact RoSPA (The Royal Society for the Prevention of Accidents) for more information and a list of road safety songs.

## Links to Foundation Stage Curriculum

**SS** Show respect for other children's personal space when playing among them (PD)

**ELG** Show awareness of space, of themselves and others (PD)

**SS** Sing a few simple, familiar songs (CD)

**SS** Begin to build a repertoire of songs (CD)

**ELG** Recognise and explore how sounds can be changed, sing simple songs from memory, recognise repeated sounds and sound patterns and match movements to music (CD)

## Health and safety

⚠ Remind children how to play the instruments safely
⚠ Ribbon sticks should have a rubber beater on the end where the ribbons are attached
⚠ Ensure that the children do not hurry or step over chairs when changing seats

# ACTIVITY 11 Singing keeps us fit!

## Resources you will need

- A puppet or large cuddly toy for the practitioner to use (the larger the better)
- A clear area for the children to be able to move freely (a perfect activity for outside)
- A chair for the 'puppeteer' to sit on
- A basket, soft bag, coloured box or similar for the puppet to appear from and go back into

## Aim/concept

- To use music and movement to teach awareness of the value of exercise

## Process

- Explain to the children that you have a special visitor who would like to meet them. Bring out the box/bag that he or she lives in.
- As discreetly as possible, put the puppet on and bring it out to sit on your lap and introduce it to the children.
- The puppet can 'speak' to the children by whispering to you. Encourage them to ask questions about it and to learn where it lives, what it likes to eat, etc.
- It can question the children through you – they will soon forget that you are there!
- Explain that the puppet has been shut up for the holidays/winter and needs some exercise to keep healthy. Start a discussion about the importance of exercise to keep us healthy and well.
- Ask the children what exercise they enjoy and how it makes them feel. Explain to the children that singing songs with actions is a really fun exercise that everyone can do!
- Begin the songs by singing 'Head, Shoulders, Knees and Toes', with the children following the puppet's actions.
- Next ask if the children would sing the puppet's favourite song, 'If You're Happy and You Know It'. Have fun by changing the words (e.g. stretch up high, cuddle your knees, jump on the spot, etc.).
- As the children become more confident, speed up, whisper the instructions, ask for suggestions, etc.
- Ask the children how they are feeling after exercising. Are they hot, sweaty, out of breath, thirsty, can they feel their hearts beating?
- Put the puppet away, remembering that puppets should be 'alive' when appearing and disappearing!
- If appropriate, allow the children to have their photograph taken with their special visitor.

## Vocabulary/discussion

- Include general questioning about the lifestyle of the puppet – where he or she lives, what he or she eats. Invite the children to introduce themselves
- Discuss exercise – why it is necessary, how it makes us feel, and examples of exercise and sports relevant to the children.
- Talk about physical changes to our bodies during exercise – sweating, becoming warmer, breathing rapidly, heart beating faster, face reddening, becoming thirsty, etc.
- Encourage the children to replace words in the songs, giving suggestions such as: 'If you're happy and you know it wiggle your toes...'

## Group size

Whole group

## Extension ideas

1. Make finger puppets to help point to body parts.
2. Introduce additional songs, for example 'I Have Ten Little Fingers', 'Here We Go Round the Mulberry Bush' (hop, skip, march, crawl, dance, etc.), adding new lyrics to old favourites (see 'Resources' on page 72).
3. Make a song book of the puppet's favourite songs.

## Links to Foundation Stage Curriculum

**SS**   Ask simple questions, often in the form of 'where' or 'what' (CLL)

**ELG**   Interact with others, negotiating plans and activities and taking turns in conversation (CLL)

**SS**   Move in a variety of ways, such as slithering, shuffling, rolling, crawling, walking, running, jumping, skipping, sliding, hopping (PD)

**ELG**   Move with confidence, imagination and in safety (PD)

**SS**   Show some understanding that good practices with regard to exercise, eating, sleeping and hygiene can contribute to good health (PD)

**ELG**   Recognise the importance of keeping healthy and those things which contribute to this

**ELG**   Recognise the changes that happen to their bodies when they are active (PD)

## Health and safety

⚠ Ensure that the children have enough space to move freely and in safety

⚠ Remind them how to avoid accidents while moving around: no running, listen to instructions, respect others, etc.

# 12 Make it rain!

## Resources you will need

- One cardboard tube per child (paper-towel roll or giftwrap inner tube)
- Heavy-duty sticky tape, such as packing tape
- Bubble wrap or tissue
- Dry rice, small beans, lentils, sand, small gravel, popcorn kernels or similar
- Funnel
- If available, a homemade rainstick or an authentic version
- A selection of paints, brushes, sponges, etc.
- Animal outlines drawn in thick marker pen and cut out for the children to paint. Use rainforest animals if possible (frogs, crocodiles, exotic birds, monkeys, snakes, etc.)

## Aim/concept

- To make a musical instrument from another country, encouraging a comparison of two cultures

## Process

- Explain to the children that they are going to make a rainstick that mimics the sounds of the rainforests where it originates. Show South America on a world map.
- Show the children your rainstick and explain that they are traditionally made from the dried wood skeleton of a cactus, which is then filled with small pebbles and used to appeal to the rain gods to send rain.
- Give each child a cardboard tube, sealed at one end.
- Help the children to push pieces of bubble wrap or tissue into the tube. Do not pack too densely, as the grains need to run through the material.
- Using a funnel, help the children to pour their chosen rice, beans, etc. into the tube. Explain that different contents will make different sounds. Discuss the sounds being created.
- When the tube is approximately half-full, seal the end with wide tape and label.
- Help the children to decorate their rainsticks using a variety of paints and pictures, which can be coloured and then stuck on.
- While they are painting, talk about the colours and the animals that they might see in the rainforest.
- When dry, display the instruments and ask each child to demonstrate his or her own.

- Ask about the sounds that they make: do they sound like rain? Do they all sound different? Which are their favourites and why? Vary the sounds by tilting them slowly and then quickly.
- See if they make the rain appear!

## Vocabulary/discussion

- Talk about South America, its location, weather, animals and plants that are found there, how we could travel there, why rain is needed, etc.
- Use comparative language when discussing the weather in the two countries: hotter/colder, wetter/drier, warmer/cooler, etc.
- Help the children to describe the rainstick: rough/smooth, light/heavy, loud/quiet, straight, long, hard/soft, shiny/matt
- Discuss the sounds of the pebbles inside – swishing, rolling, rainy, hissing, tapping, spraying, falling, etc.

## Group size

3–4

## Extension ideas

1. Link to activities about the weather.
2. Use the rainsticks during songs about the weather and rain.
3. Compare the rainsticks to other percussion instruments. What are the similarities/differences?
4. Find out where other instruments originate.

## Links to Foundation Stage Curriculum

**SS** Build up vocabulary that reflects the breadth of their experiences (CLL)

**ELG** Extend their vocabulary, exploring the meanings and sounds of new words (CLL)

**SS** Show an interest in the world in which they live (KUW)

**ELG** Observe, find out about and identify features in the place they live and the natural world (KUW)

**ELG** Find out about their environment, and talk about those features they like and dislike (KUW)

**SS** Make three-dimensional structures (CD)

**SS** Make constructions, collages, paintings, drawings and dances (CD)

**ELG** Explore colour, texture, shape, form and space in two or three dimensions (CD)

## Health and safety

⚠ Supervise process closely and clean up spills immediately

⚠ All paint to be non-toxic

⚠ Remind children not to put rainstick contents in their mouths, noses, etc.

⚠ Beans and corn kernels etc. may cause slipping hazard if they fall on the floor, so sweep up thoroughly

**ACTIVITY 13**

# 'Why does the butterfly flutterby?'

## Resources you will need

- Pictures and photographs of caterpillars and butterflies
- A real butterfly and/or caterpillar (if available)
- Music player and a recording of 'When I'm a Butterfly' (see photocopiable sheet 9 on page 66)
- A selection of silk scarves or fabric pieces suitable for use as butterfly wings (a brass ring may be sewn onto a corner to loop their fingers through)
- Space for the children to move freely (a perfect activity for outdoors)

## Aim/concept

- To enjoy music and movement, imitating movements of familiar creatures and singing a song about them

## Process

- You may wish to familiarise the children with the butterfly song during previous sessions.
- Talk to the children about caterpillars and butterflies.
- Look at and talk about any pictures that you may have showing these creatures. In particular discuss how they move.
- Explain to the children that they are going to be very clever and turn themselves into butterflies from caterpillars.
- Play some music which will help the children to move around their space as a caterpillar would. Encourage them to wriggle on their tummies, roll over, shuffle forwards and backwards, etc. (see pages 69 and 70).
- Children who are less physically able may wish to make caterpillar movements with their finger in their hand and may make wing movements while sitting if necessary.
- Ask the children what they will need to fly and transform themselves into butterflies and let them choose two wing scarves.
- Play the 'When I'm a Butterfly' song and encourage them to fly by flapping their wings up and down and moving gently and freely within their space, being considerate to others.
- Move among them, draping your wings over their faces as they move past and copying their movements as you all sing the song.

## Vocabulary/discussion

- Discuss caterpillars and butterflies, where they live, what they eat, how they move, etc.
- What do they like and dislike about caterpillars and butterflies?
- Explore the differences between the two creatures
- Use words to describe the music that you have chosen: light, airy, floaty, happy, springtime, etc.
- How did it make the children feel?

## Group size

Whole group

## Extension ideas

1. Silk paint or tie-dye the fabric squares to make colourful wings.
2. Read *The Very Hungry Caterpillar* by Eric Carle (Hamish Hamilton).
3. Link to activities about butterflies, insects, nature, spring, gardens, etc.
4. Paint their own butterflies by folding shapes in half, butterfly printing.

## Links to Foundation Stage Curriculum

**SS** Describe simple features of objects and events (KUW)

**SS** Examine objects and living things to find out more about them (KUW)

**ELG** Investigate objects and materials by using all of their senses as appropriate (KUW)

**ELG** Find out about, and identify, some features of living things, objects and events they observe (KUW)

**SS** Manage body to create intended movements (PD)

**SS** Combine and repeat a range of movements (PD)

**ELG** Move with control and coordination

**ELG** Travel around, under, over and through balancing and climbing equipment (PD)

**SS** Imitate and create movement in response to music (CD)

**ELG** Recognise and explore how sounds can be changed, sing simple songs from memory, recognise repeated sounds and sound patterns and match movements to music (CD)

## Health and safety

⚠ Ensure that the children do not become too boisterous when moving about

⚠ Make sure that the children have adequate room to move

⚠ Surfaces must not be slippery, especially if outside

# ACTIVITY 14 Find a friend

## Resources you will need

- Adequate space to stand in a large circle
- A mat or small chair
- A blanket

## Aim/concept

- To introduce ring games and basic rhythm

## Process

- Explain to the children that they are going to play a singing game where they have to guess who is under the blanket.
- Sit the children in a large circle with the mat or chair in the middle.
- Starting with yourself, say your name slowly while clapping out the syllables,

    For example:    MISS CHAM – BER – LAIN (4 CLAPS)

- Go around the class and help them to clap their names. If they cannot clap the syllables, allow them to call out their name.

    Examples:    VIC – TOR – I – A (4 CLAPS)
    BEN – JA – MIN (3 CLAPS)

- Ask the children to shut their eyes and sit one of the group silently under a blanket on the mat. If they are unhappy under the blanket, stand them behind it.
- With eyes open, sing the following song as a group, clapping along if you wish:

    Come and play, join our game,
    Be our friend and say your name,
    Come and play and join our game,
    Be our friend and say your name!

    (To the tune of 'This Old Man')

- Lead the children in guessing the name of the child and ask the child in the middle to say yes or no to the guesses. Add some unlikely ones – the children will love it!
- Allow everyone to take a turn if they wish.
- At the end of the game, go around the circle once more and clap the syllables of GOOD – BYE, followed by their names again.

For example   GOOD – BYE ZI – A (4 CLAPS)
GOOD – BYE JOHN (3 CLAPS)

This method can be used when taking the register on a daily basis.
- To celebrate birthdays, use the same set-up but perhaps decorate the chair by draping with gold or silver material or tying a balloon to the chair. Sit the birthday child on the chair and place a crown or tiara on his/her head before singing 'Happy Birthday to You'.

## Vocabulary/discussion

- According to the children's stage of development, introduce the word 'syllable' and begin to break words into syllables
- Encourage repetition of basic song words

## Group size

Whole group

## Extension ideas

1. Sing other ring songs such as 'Hokey Cokey', 'Here We Go Round the Mulberry Bush', 'There Was a Princess Long Ago', 'The Big Ship Sails on the Alley, Alley O' (see 'Resources' on page 72).
2. Clap the syllables of objects around the room (e.g. colours, shapes, etc.), choosing words of different lengths.
3. Make up different patterns such as PUR – PLE, PUR – PLE, PINK, RED, IN – DI – GO.
4. Slowly clap the syllables to a simple rhyme or song. Have fun getting faster as the children grasp the concept.

## Links to Foundation Stage Curriculum

| SS | Enjoy rhyming and rhythmic activities (CLL) |
| ELG | Hear and say initial and final sounds in words, and short vowel sounds within words (CLL) |
| ELG | Link sounds to letters, naming and sounding the letters of the alphabet (CLL) |
| ELG | Use their phonic knowledge to write simple regular words and make phonetically plausible attempts at more complex words (CLL) |
| SS | Enjoy joining in with dancing and ring games (CD) |
| SS | Tap out simple repeated rhythms and make some up (CD) |
| ELG | Recognise and explore how sounds can be changed, sing simple songs from memory, recognise repeated sounds and sound patterns and match movements to music (CD) |

## Health and safety

⚠ Be aware that some children may not like to be covered with a blanket. Use it as a screen instead

# ACTIVITY 15 Ribbon sticks

## Resources you will need

- One rubber-ended beater per child
- A selection of pieces of brightly coloured ribbon approximately 50 cm long
- Music player and selection of music of varying tempos (see pages 69–70 for suggestions)

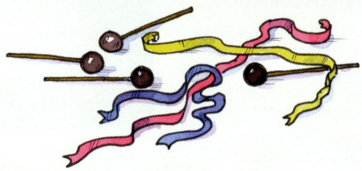

## Aim/concept

- To move in different ways to music that has a variety of tempos and styles

## Process

- Explain to the children that they are going to make a ribbon stick, which they will use to create different patterns to music.
- Show them a ready-made version and ask them to watch carefully as you play the first piece of music selected from the 'Relaxing/calming' category on page 69.
- Move the ribbon stick to the music and then discuss the movements.
- Play the second piece selected from the 'Energising' category on page 70, using more exaggerated, bolder movements with the ribbon stick.
- Discuss the second piece and the movements that you made, asking the children how it made them feel.
- Help them to make their own ribbon sticks by selecting ribbon lengths and tying them to the beaters at the rubber end.
- Ensure that the children have plenty of space and play contrasting pieces of music for them to move their ribbon sticks to. Stress the importance of not poking the ribbon sticks into other children and respecting each other's space, as they make both bold and gentle movements.
- Finish by singing a song about making shapes to music (see Photocopiable sheet 10 on page 67).

## Vocabulary/discussion

- Explore emotions experienced while listening to music: happy/sad, excited, energetic/relaxed, bold, lively, strong, dramatic, etc.
- Discuss patterns created with the ribbon sticks: flowing, wavy, spiral, circular, zigzag, jagged, large/small, up/down, straight/curvy, etc.
- Identify language used when making the sticks: tying a knot, lengths of ribbon, equal length, uneven/even, amount, secure firmly, slide off, etc.
- Share song words

## Group size

Whole group

## Extension ideas

1. Observe and copy each other's actions, as a group and in pairs.
2. Help the children to paint the shapes that they create with their ribbon sticks, or to stick wool or string to paper to form the different shapes. Display.
3. Create a dance using whole body movements to a favourite piece of music.

## Links to Foundation Stage Curriculum

| | |
|---|---|
| **SS** | Have an awareness of the boundaries set and behavioural expectations within the setting (PSE) |
| **ELG** | Understand what is right, what is wrong, and why |
| **ELG** | Consider the consequences of their words and actions for themselves and others (PSE) |
| **SS** | Begin to use anticlockwise movement and retrace vertical lines (CLL) |
| **ELG** | Use a pencil and hold it effectively to form recognisable letters, most of which are correctly formed (CLL) |
| **SS** | Respond to sound with body movement (CD) |
| **SS** | Begin to move rhythmically (CD) |
| **ELG** | Recognise and explore how sounds can be changed, sing simple songs from memory, recognise repeated sounds and sound patterns and match movements to music (CD) |

## Health and safety

⚠ Take care when using lengths of ribbon
⚠ Tie the ribbons onto the rubber end of the beater to avoid poking into faces etc.
⚠ Demonstrate safe use before commencing

## ACTIVITY 16   Musical bodies

### Resources you will need

- Tape recorder and cassette (optional)

---

### Aim/concept

- To use body percussion to introduce rhythm patterns

---

### Process

- Sit the children in a circle, explaining to the group that you are going to be making music using their bodies as instruments.
- Ask for suggestions and give some examples, e.g. clapping hands, tapping two fingers on palm, stamping, saying 'shh', finger to lips, 'popping' cheeks full of air, clucking with tongue, tapping knees with open hands, etc.
- Begin by clapping the syllables to their names as you move around the circle (see Activity 14).
- Sing the song 'If You're Happy and You Know It' but adapt it to use the children's names, encouraging them to identify themselves by using various body percussion sounds.

  > For example:    'If you're Daniel and you know it, clap your hands'
  > *(Daniel claps)*
  > 'If you're Deepa and you know it, stamp your feet'
  > *(Deepa stamps)*

- Ask the group to copy the sequence, making the sequences longer and more complicated as appropriate.
- Ask the children to make up their own sequences for you to copy. Include some planned errors for the children to enjoy catching you out!
- Depending on the group size and stage of development, you may wish to try the sequences in pairs or small groups.
- The children may find it interesting to use the tape recorder to record their sequences and to play them back to check them.

## Vocabulary/discussion

- Talk about parts of the body and the sounds created for percussion – clapping, stamping, stomping, rubbing, clicking, tapping, etc.
- Explain how to use the tape player – rewind, play, fast forward, record, etc.
- Memorise simple songs

## Group size

Whole group or 4–6 : 1

## Extension ideas

1. Clap to the beat of familiar songs. Replace one word per line with body percussion, e.g. 'I hear *clap clap*, I hear *clap clap*, hark don't *pop*, hark don't *pop*, pitter patter *stamp stamp*, etc.
2. Divide the group into teams (each led by a practitioner) and see which team can copy the sequences most accurately.
3. Cut out and paint a large body shape and attach labels to it naming all the body percussion sounds that you made. Display.

## Links to Foundation Stage Curriculum

**SS** Manage body to create intended movements (PD)

**SS** Combine and repeat a range of movements (PD)

**ELG** Move with control and coordination (PD)

**ELG** Travel around, under, over and through balancing and climbing equipment (PD)

**SS** Tap out simple repeated rhythms and make some up (CD)

**ELG** Recognise and explore how sounds can be changed, sing simple songs from memory, recognise repeated sounds and sound patterns and match movements to music (CD)

## Health and safety

⚠ No specific issues to be taken into consideration

# ACTIVITY 17 Colour-coded percussion

## Resources you will need

- A selection of percussion instruments
- Coloured dots to stick on the instruments
- Discussion resources (see pages 9–18)
- An A4-sized basic 'book', containing blank pages to record sequences
- Coloured discs to stick in the book to record sequences

## Aim/concept

- To introduce the children to musical notes and to show how instruments play and rest

## Process

- Sit the children around a table which has a selection of percussion instruments in the middle. Ask them to choose an instrument and place a coloured dot on it (different colour for each child).
- For a whole-group activity, divide into smaller groups and allocate each group member the same colour-coded instrument, e.g. red table play castanets, blue table play hand bells, etc.
- Explain how music is written as notes instead of words. Show them an example on photocopiable sheet 11 (page 68). (Sheet music is written on lines arranged in groups of five, with musical notes marked as a dot on, above or below the line.)
- Explain how instruments sometimes remain quiet during songs. Ask them to play their instruments together, individually and then to hold them still.
- Adapt the words to sing about each instrument so that every child takes a turn.
- Ask the children to listen carefully as you call out a sequence of the colours, e.g. red, blue, yellow, green, blue, etc.
- Help them to play their instruments in that sequence. Stick discs into the book as they play and show them how they are making their own tunes.
- Vary sequences and record in their book as they play them.
- Display the book and a selection of the colour-coded instruments for the children to use at a later date.

## Vocabulary/discussion

- Identify correct names of all the percussion instruments
- Use language relating to music: notes, note names, sheet music, etc.
- Share song words
- Discuss colours used and words such as sequence, record, tunes, patterns

## Group size

4–6 or whole group

## Extension ideas

1. As their confidence grows, ask the children to call out colour/instrument sequences.
2. 'Challenge' other practitioners to come and try to play the sequences using the children's 'music book' and colour-coded instruments.
3. As a small group activity, help the children to stick coloured discs into the book as they play sequences.

## Links to Foundation Stage Curriculum

**SS** Listen to favourite nursery rhymes, stories and songs. Join in with repeated refrains, anticipating key events and important phrases (CLL)

**SS** Respond to simple instructions (CLL)

**ELG** Enjoy listening to and using spoken and written language, and readily turn to it in their play and learning (CLL)

**ELG** Sustain attentive listening, responding to what they have heard by relevant comments, questions or actions (CLL)

**ELG** Listen with enjoyment, and respond to stories, songs and other music, rhymes and poems and make up their own stories, songs, rhymes and poems (CLL)

**SS** Choose particular colours to use for a purpose (CD)

**ELG** Explore colour, texture, shape, form and space in two or three dimensions (CD)

## Health and safety

⚠ Remind the children how to play percussion instruments safely and correctly

## ACTIVITY 18 Making music

### Resources you will need

- Examples of sheet music (see photocopiable sheet 11 on page 68, or go to www.8notes.com for blank sheets)
- Large cut-outs of various notes (see the photograph opposite for examples; black sugar paper, approximately A5 size, works best)
- A long piece of wallpaper lining paper with music lines drawn across it in thick black pen to resemble a five-line stave (see www.8notes.com for examples)
- Glue
- White chalk
- A selection of percussion instruments

### Aim/concept

- To introduce the children to sheet music and to create their own

### Process

- Explain to the children that music is written down using notes rather than words. Ask if they have seen it before (show examples on photocopiable page 11) and how it differs from their books.
- Explain that some of the notes are up high and some are down low. Ask them to copy you as you sing the word high in a high voice and low in a lower voice.
- Help them to choose an instrument and to play it up high and down low – up with the birds and down with the worms!
- Sing a familiar song and ask the children to copy you as you play the instruments up high and down low. Depending on their stage of development, alter the pitch as you sing.
- Show the children your large sheet of music paper and help them to choose a note to stick onto it. Encourage them to place some notes higher and some lower.
- Write their name on their note in white chalk and display.

## Vocabulary/discussion

- Introduce words linked to music, e.g. notes, note names, sheet music, tunes, lines, dots, squiggles, symbols, high/low, higher/lower
- Compare books to music, e.g. notes instead of words, no pictures or colours

## Group size

Whole group

## Extension ideas

1. Invite the children to sing their favourite songs in a high/low voice as they get used to the concept.
2. Decide which instruments are high or low, e.g. a triangle sounds higher than a drum.
3. Show how a xylophone or piano has high and low notes.

## Links to Foundation Stage Curriculum

| | |
|---|---|
| ELG | Talk about, recognise and recreate simple patterns (MD) |
| ELG | Use language such as 'circle' or 'bigger' to describe the shape and size of solids and flat shapes (MD) |
| ELG | Use everyday words to describe position (MD) |
| ELG | Use developing mathematical ideas and methods to solve practical problems (MD) |
| SS | Differentiate marks and movements on paper (CD) |
| SS | Understand that different media can be combined (CD) |
| ELG | Explore colour, texture, shape, form and space in two or three dimensions (CD) |

## Health and safety

- ⚠ Ensure that suitable glue is used carefully in a protected area
- ⚠ Clean up spills immediately
- ⚠ Wash hands after using glue
- ⚠ Instruments should be played carefully, beaters kept away from eyes and faces and never be put in mouths

# Photocopiable sheets

# How to make an Old Lady puppet

## Resources you will need

- One adult-sized sock
- Wool for hair and large embroidery needle
- Stick-on plastic eyes or felt pieces to stick on as eyes
- PVA glue
- A rubber band

## Process

- Place the sock over one hand. Place the rubber band over the sock and across your palm to create the mouth when you press fingers and thumb together.
- Curve your fingers on the puppet hand towards you and place the eyes on the top of the sock where your knuckles are.
- Attach hair strands above the eyes by threading wool through the sock fabric in large loops, or sticking pieces of wool next to each other just above the eyes. Make it as long and shaggy as you wish.
- Practise 'feeding' small plastic or felt animals into the puppet's mouth, or draw and laminate cardboard animals for the children to 'feed' to her.
- You may wish to help the children to create their own Old Lady puppet once you have mastered your own.

# Song words – 'There Was an Old Lady'

There was an old lady who swallowed a fly
I don't know why she swallowed a fly – perhaps she'll die!

There was an old lady who swallowed a spider,
That wriggled and wriggled and wriggled inside her;
She swallowed the spider to catch the fly;
I don't know why she swallowed a fly – perhaps she'll die!

There was an old lady who swallowed a bird;
How absurd to swallow a bird.
She swallowed the bird to catch the spider,
She swallowed the spider to catch the fly;
I don't know why she swallowed a fly – perhaps she'll die!

There was an old lady who swallowed a cat;
Fancy that to swallow a cat!
She swallowed the cat to catch the bird,
She swallowed the bird to catch the spider,
She swallowed the spider to catch the fly;
I don't know why she swallowed a fly – perhaps she'll die!

There was an old lady who swallowed a dog;
What a hog, to swallow a dog;
She swallowed the dog to catch the cat,
She swallowed the cat to catch the bird,
She swallowed the bird to catch the spider,
She swallowed the spider to catch the fly;
I don't know why she swallowed a fly – perhaps she'll die!

There was an old lady who swallowed a horse . . .
She's dead, of course!

# Song words –
# 'Naan Bread in the Oven'

Naan bread in the oven,
Naan bread in the oven,
Tear it, taste it,
Tear it, taste it,
Naan bread in the oven!

Pasta on your plate,
Pasta on your plate,
Wind it round,
Wind it round,
Pasta on your plate!

Stir fry in your wok,
Stir fry in your wok,
Sizzle, sizzle,
Sizzle, sizzle,
Stir fry in your wok!

Curry in the pot,
Curry in the pot,
Nice 'n' spicy,
Nice 'n' spicy
Curry in the pot!

Sing to the tune of 'Jelly on a Plate' and see if the children can suggest alternatives, e.g. pancakes in a pan, sausage on the grill, bananas in the bowl, etc.

Use the illustrations below to create your own stickers.

Encourage the children to choose the expression that resembles their feelings in Activity 2.

Happy

Sad

Angry

Afraid

Surprised

Sleepy

(Ilustrations are reproduced from *Learning Through Phonics*, Collette Drifte (2003), David Fulton Publishers.

© Julie Durno (2006) *Music and Singing*, published by David Fulton Publishers Ltd.

# Lullaby time

The following songs would be suitable for use in Activity 4:

Rock-a-bye Baby
Hush Little Baby
Golden Slumbers
Mary Had a Little Lamb
Pat-a-cake
Twinkle, Twinkle Little Star
Humpty Dumpty
Hickory Dickory Dock
Row, Row, Row Your Boat
Baa Baa Black Sheep
Are You Sleeping?
Kumbaya
My Bonnie Lies Over the Ocean
Polly Put the Kettle On
Miss Polly Had a Dolly
Incy Wincy Spider
Ring-a-ring-a-roses

## Classical pieces

*Sleeping Beauty* – Tchaikovsky
*Cradle Song* – Julian Lloyd Webber
*Swan Lake* – Tchaikovsky
*The Magic Flute* – Mozart
*Für Elise* – Beethoven
*Lullaby* – Brahms

Tapes and CDs can be found in libraries and charity shops, or bought from bookshops or online at www.kidsmusic.co.uk or www.sleeplullabies.com.

Words can be found in *This Little Puffin* by Elizabeth Matterson (Puffin) and purchased at www.penguin.com

Song words can also be found at www.bussongs.com

# Counting songs

## 1, 2, 3, 4, 5 Once I Caught a Fish Alive

1, 2, 3, 4, 5
*(Count on fingers)*
Once I caught a fish alive,
*(Wriggle fingers like a fish)*
6, 7, 8, 9, 10
*(Count on fingers)*
Then I let him go again,
*(Pretend to throw fish back)*
Why did you let him go,
Because he bit my finger so,
*(Show finger)*
Which finger did he bite?
This little finger on my right!
*(Hold up and wriggle finger)*

## Five Currant Buns in a Baker's Shop

Five currant buns in a baker's shop,
Big and round with sugar on the top,
Along came Anna with a penny to pay,
Bought a currant bun and took it away.

*(Repeat, lowering the numbers and changing the children's names.)*

## Ten Fat Sausages Sizzling in a Pan

Ten fat sausages sizzling in a pan,
One went pop and then it went BANG!

*(Repeat, lowering the numbers and using
tambourines or drums for the pop and bang.)*

(Lyrics from 'Counting songs' tape, available from Kidsmusic.)

# Counting songs

## This Old Man

This old man,
He played one,
He played nick–nack on my drum
With a nick–nack paddy whack,
Give a dog a bone,
This old man came rolling home.

Two:      on my shoe
Three:    on my knee
Four:     on my door
Five:     on my hive
Six:      on my sticks
Seven:    down in Devon
Eight:    on my gate
Nine:     on my sign
Ten:      once again

## The Ants Went Marching

The ants went marching
One by one, hurrah, hurrah,
The ants went marching
One by one, hurrah, hurrah
The ants went marching one by one,
The little one stopped to suck his thumb,
And they all went marching in to get out of the rain.

Two by two: stopped to do up his shoe
Three by three: stopped to climb a tree
Four by four: stopped to shut the door
Five by five: stopped to say goodbye

(Lyrics from 'Counting songs' tape, available from Kidsmusic.)

# Counting songs

## Ten Little Toys

Ten little toys
In my toybox shut
Shall we tidy, tidy them all up?
Open the lid
And one runs away
Nine are left for me to play!

*(Repeat until none are left, to the tune of 'Five Currant Buns in a Baker's Shop.)*

## Five Little Leaves

Five little leaves so bright and gay
Were dancing about on a tree one day.
The wind came blowing through the town
Whooooooooo . . . Whooooooooo
And one little leaf came tumbling down

Four little leaves etc.

(© *This Little Puffin*, Elizabeth Matterson (1997), Penguins Reproduced by permission of the publishers.)

*(Sing to tune of 'Five Little Ducks', with children moving fingers like leaves, or turning bodies with arms outstretched. Blow through cupped hands for sounds, or use shakers, shake tambourines, turn rainsticks, shake bags of silver foil or dried leaves, etc.)*

## One Man Went to Mow

One man went to mow,
Went to mow a meadow,
One man and his dog, Patch,
Went to mow a meadow.

Two men went to mow, etc.

*(Encourage the children to suggest new names for the dog each verse. It is also fun to change 'one man' for a child's name.)*

# Song words – 'When I'm a Butterfly'

I'm not good looking
I'm not a pretty sight
Eating and crawling, I'll give you quite a fright!
Caterpillars look ferocious
To keep the birds away
And all the other creatures
Who think of me as prey.

CHORUS:
But when I'm a butterfly, I'll flutterby,
I'll soar in the air and fly in the sky
And you won't believe it's me.
When I'm a butterfly, without a lie,
I'll be so lovely, no longer ugly,
What a pretty thing I'll be.

I'm always hungry
I must have lots to eat
Delicious green leaves, that's what I call a treat.
Caterpillars in the garden
Growing day by day
Then to your amazement
We'll change and fly away!

(Repeat chorus)

(Available on Incy Wincy Spider Tape and CD available from CYP Children's Audio Company: www.kidsmusic.co.uk)

# Ribbon stick songs

## Making shapes

We are making spirals all day,
We are making spirals all day,
We are making spirals,
We are making spirals,
We are making spirals, all day.

*Variations:*

We are making circles all day...
We are making zigzags all day...
We are making triangles all day...

*(Sing to the tune of 'Train Is a Coming, Oh Yeah')*

## This is the way...

This is the way we wave up high,
Wave up high,
Wave up high,
This is the way we wave up high,
When we use our ribbon sticks.

*Variations:*

This is the way we crouch down low...
This is the way we make a spiral...
This is the way we zigzag fast...

*(Sing to the tune of 'This Is the Way We Put on Our Coats')*

The children will have plenty of suggestions of their own, and other favourite songs can be adapted in this way.

# Example of sheet music

# Choosing music to accompany the activities

Once you start to enjoy music with the children, you will learn which types of music work well and become favourites.

Build up your own collection, look out for bargains in charity shops, car boot sales, library sales and so on. National newspapers and magazines often give away CDs of various music, often on a theme, e.g. relaxing or summer sounds. Parents and carers may also provide old tapes and CDs to add to the collection.

The following pieces are suggestions and the list is by no means exhaustive, but these have worked well for me during trials of the activities in the book.

Those marked * worked well during Activity 13, when the children needed to move like caterpillars to music.

## Relaxing/calming

Faure – *Pavane*
Mozart – Piano concerto No. 21 (2nd mov't) (*Elvira Madigan*)*
Mascagni – Intermezzo from *Cavalleria Rusticana*
Massenet – Meditation from *Thaïs*
Pachelbel – *Canon*
Dvorak – Symphony No. 9 (2nd mov't) ('From the New World')
Bach – Suite No. 3, Air

## Majestic, dramatic

Handel – *Water Music,* Hornpipe
Wagner – *Lohengrin*, prelude to Act 3
Holst – *The Planets*, 'Mars'
Handel – *Messiah (Hallelujah Chorus)*
Strauss – Emperor Waltz
Elgar – *Pomp and Circumstance* marches

## Uplifting, cheerful, lighthearted

Strauss – *Die Fledermaus* (laughing song)
Vivaldi – 'Spring'* from *The Four Seasons*
Holst – *The Planets*, 'Jupiter'
Beethoven – Piano Concerto no. 1 (3rd mov't)

## Romantic

Rodrigo – *Concierto de Aranjuez* (2nd mov't)
Rachmaninov – Rhapsody on a Theme of Paganini (18th variation)
(graceful, contemplative)
Tchaikovsky – *The Nutcracker, Waltz of the Flowers*
Chopin – Nocturne in E flat major

## Energising

Strauss – 'Thunder and Lightning' Polka (good for weather activities)
Verdi – *Requiem* (Dies Irae)
Verdi – Chorus of the Hebrew Slaves (*Nabucco*)
Orff – *Carmina Burana*, 'O Fortuna' (sounds like a storm at sea)
Wagner – 'Ride of the Valkyries' (*Die Walküre*) (very dramatic)

## Sad

Elgar – Cello Concerto (for slow movements, sombre, winter/night)
Albinoni – Adagio
Mahler – Symphony No. 5, Adagietto
Ravel – *Pavane for a Dead Princess*
Grieg – *Peer Gynt* (Solveig's song)

A music company called Global Journey (www.globaljourney.com)
has a wonderful range of music from around the world. Here are some
examples:

Eternal Flames – Native American Indian
Boanns Clan – Dance of the Water Gods (Irish dance music and songs)
'Celtic Sanctuary' – Irish music including Uillean Pipes, Harps and Penny
Whistles
Born Free – African drum beats, captivating rhythms
Spirit of India – Music from Asia

Ulara – A tribute to the indigenous people of Australia
Caribbean Steel Drum rhythms
CDs from France, Latin America and Egypt
There are also CDs and tapes of sounds from nature, including:

Whalesong
Rainforest
The Sea
Birdsong

These work well during music sessions, or during topical activities.

# Resources

## Useful resources and suppliers

Puppets by Post (a division of The Puppet Company Ltd), Units 2–4 Cam Centre, Wilbury Way, Hitchin, Hertfordshire SG4 0TW (01462 446040 www.puppetsbypost.com) are a friendly, helpful company who supply over 1,000 beautiful puppets of every description.

NES Arnold (www.nesarnold.co.uk) sells a wide range of percussion instruments and musical toys and games suitable for early years. They are safe and durable and can be bought in bulk.

*This Little Puffin*, compiled by Elizabeth Matterson (Puffin) (www.penguin.com), is a delightful book that contains the words and music to many popular traditional and modern songs.

*The Very Hungry Caterpillar* by Eric Carle (Hamish Hamilton) would be a good book to read as an extension to Activity 13 and is available from good bookshops and www.amazon.co.uk

RoSPA (The Royal Society for the Prevention of Accidents) have a series of road safety songs and may provide supporting literature (www.rospa.co.uk).

OXFAM sell toys and instruments from around the world (check for safety before using).

Toybox Crafts Ltd are a charity based in Amersham, Buckinghamshire selling products from around the world with profits going to Guatemala to help their street children (01494 432591 www.solidsecurityonline.com/~toybox/acatalog/info.html). Craft packs are available and a catalogue containing some beautiful shakers, authentic rainsticks, pan flutes etc. Contact Hazel Simpson on hazel.simpson@toybox.org

Music Education Services Ltd provide a wide range of instruments, posters and resources to schools and pre-schools. Contact them at music.mes@btinternet.com, 020 8770 3866 or 101 Banstead Road South, Sutton, Surrey, SM2 5LH.

## Websites

www.puppetsbypost.com will send a catalogue of their delightful puppets free of charge.

www.kidsmusic.co.uk is a good website to find a wide variety of children's music.

www.sleeplullabies.com have many sleep related songs and music.

www.bussongs.com can provide the words to many popular children's songs.

www.Cdconnection.com have a wide selection of world music, including South American.

www.amazon.co.uk have a wide selection of books and music for children.

www.8notes.com has blank music paper (5 line staves) that you could print off to show the children.

www.galt-educational.co.uk have a comprehensive range of quality educational supplies.

www.hope-education.co.uk supply quality educational supplies and instruments.